Growing Things

David Marshall

Macdonald

How to use this book

First, look at the contents page opposite. Read the list to see if it includes the subject you want. The list tells you what each page is about, and you can find the page with the information you need.

In the book, some words are **darker** than the others. These are harder words. Sometimes, there is a picture to explain the word. For example, the word **carpel** appears on page 9 and there is a picture of it on page 9. Other words are explained in the word list on page 30.

Some pages in the book contain a computer activity. If you want to try the activity take the matching card from the pocket at the back of the book. Read the card and follow the instructions with care.

Educational Consultants:
Heather Govier
Diana Robinson
Factual Consultant:
Adam Cade

Editor: Daphne Butler
Designer: Ewing Paddock
Picture Research: Kathy Lockley
Production: Ken Holt

Illustrators: Teresa O'Brien 8-9, 10-11, 14-15, 18, 20-21, 22, 25
Maggie Raynor 12-13, 16-17, 19, 28-29

Photographs:
Heather Angel, Biofotos 20-21
Robert Harding Picture Library 9, 11, 16-17, 24-25, 26-27B, 27
Spectrum Colour Library 6-7, 8, 12-13, 18-19, 22-23, 26-27T

Programming Assistants:
Nigel Scott (BBC B)
Michael Headley (RML 480Z)

A MACDONALD BOOK

First published in Great Britain in 1986 by
Macdonald & Co (Publishers) Ltd
London & Sydney
A BPCC plc Company

ISBN 0 356 11577 1

Printed and bound in Great Britain by
William Clowes Limited, Beccles and London

Macdonald & Co (Publishers) Ltd
Greater London House, Hampstead Road
London NW1 7QX

CONTENTS

The growing world

Look out of your window. Wherever you live, there are likely to be lots of different plants nearby. These will be all shapes and sizes. Some are very surprising.

Plants need some rain and some sunshine before they can grow, and they need some soil for the roots to grow into. There are only a few plants that are able to grow in the very cold parts of the world like the North and South Poles, or in the very hot deserts.

Hundreds of millions of years ago the plants that were growing in the shallow water near the sea shores began to get closer and closer to the land. At last they were growing right out of the water, slowly taking over the land. Plants were the first living things on land.

To begin with all plants, from the smallest moss to the biggest tree, grew wild undisturbed by people. As animals and people developed they fed on the plants. Later, people found out how to use plants in other ways. They used wood to make their houses, and discovered how to make medicines from plants. They made fires out of wood to cook their food and to keep themselves warm.

What makes a plant?

Everything that grows upwards from the ground is a plant. In your garden there may be bulbs, flowers and vegetables, grass, bushes and trees. They are all green plants.

Although there are so many types of plants they all have the same parts. Almost every plant has roots, a stem, leaves, a flower and seeds.

If you look at a buttercup, a cabbage and a fir tree you will see that the parts of a plant can be many different shapes and sizes.

Brightly coloured flowers attract insects

Why do plants need bees and butterflies?

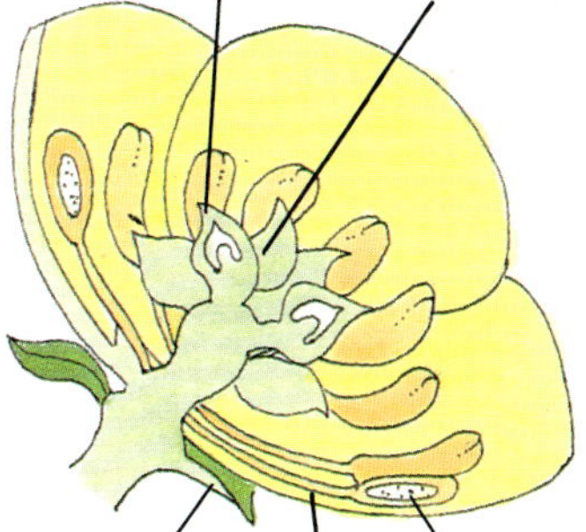

Most flowers have petals, which are usually the brightly coloured parts. Below the petals there are often green bits which were wrapped around the bud before the flower came out. These are called **sepals.**

Inside the flower, next to the petals are the male bits or **stamens.** These produce the **pollen**, that is the powder that can rub off on to your fingers. In the middle of the flower is the female bit or **carpel**. Some flowers have more than one carpel. At the bottom of each carpel is the part of the plant that holds the seeds and grows into the fruit.

Seeds will only grow if they are dusted with pollen. There is a little stalk in the centre of the flower, part of the carpel, called the **stigma**. The sticky pad at the end of this stalk catches the pollen. Some pollen is scattered by the wind and some is carried by insects. The petals of some flowers are brightly coloured to attract these insects.

The seed story . . .

Have you ever grown mustard seeds on wet kitchen paper? Can you remember what happens . . .?

First the water soaks into the seed. The seed gets very soft and it swells up. Inside the seed is a baby plant with its own store of food. When the water soaks into the seed the baby plant (or **germ**) uses the food to start growing (**germinating**).

The baby plant pushes a root downwards through an opening in the skin of the seed. With the help of water found by the root a stem starts to grow. This pushes upwards looking for sunlight. Small green leaves soon appear on the stem.

Now, with the help of the green leaves, the plant can make its own food. It uses the sunlight and the air, and the soil water that the roots find, and it grows bigger and bigger and bigger . . .

Mustard plants

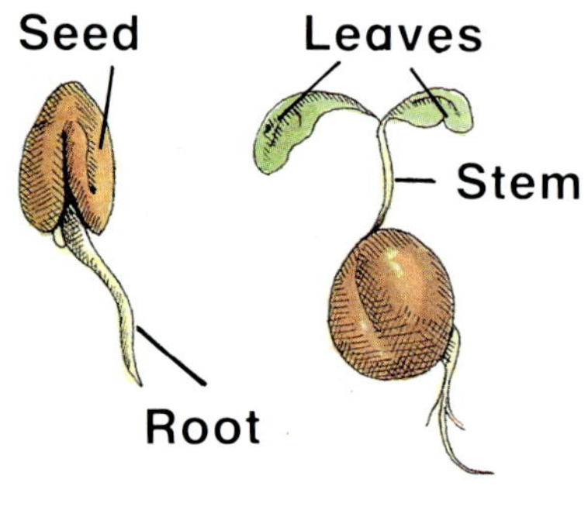

Some seeds are very small and light. They blow around in the wind. Some of them will land in good soil and grow. Other seeds are carried by insects and animals. Birds often carry berries and drop parts of them on the ground.

People sometimes get seeds on their shoes when they are walking through fields of long grass. Perhaps you have planted some seeds without knowing it!

COMPUTER ACTIVITY 1

The Computer Activity cards are at the back of the book. The first one is about something that grows when most seeds sprout - a leaf.

You can make a leaf. Then change its colour. You can even make a leaf garden with lots of leaves of different colours.

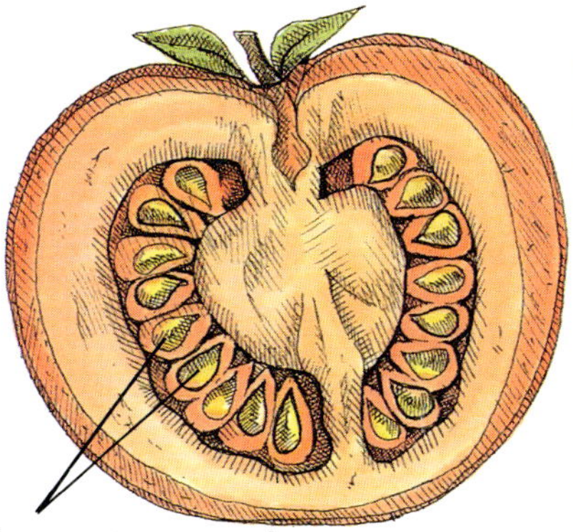

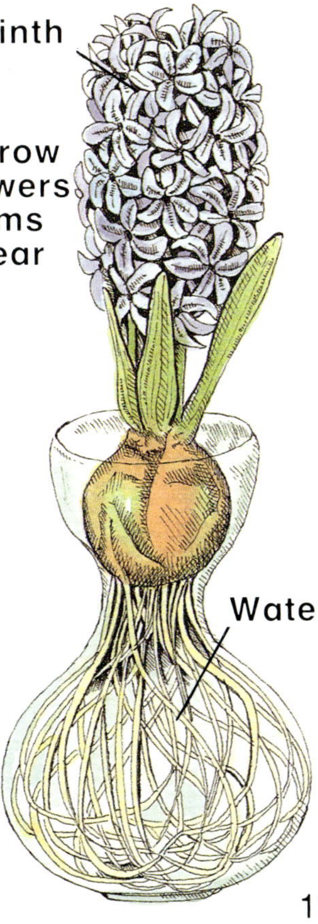

Most seeds need to grow in soil. You can plant seeds outside in the ground, or indoors in pots. You could try collecting seeds from a tomato fruit and planting them in a pot. You must keep the soil warm and damp and, perhaps, you will grow a tomato plant.

Growing wild

Bluebells

There are wild flowers all over the world. We only get our colourful wild flowers in the spring and summer, but in some hot and wet parts of the world they grow all the time.

One of our best known wild flowers is the dandelion. They have pretty yellow flowers, and later fluffy seed heads.

You can use the flowers to make wine. The leaves make a good salad, but beware, you must first wash off the taste of car petrol fumes, if you collected the dandelion leaves by the roadside! The roots make a medicine and a drink that tastes like coffee. Some people say it is better!

Many of the first medicines were made from plants, and some are still used today.

People in great pain are given **morphine** which comes from poppies. People who have heart troubles are given **digitoxin**; it comes from the foxglove. **Quinine** cures people who get an awful disease called **malaria**. **Aspirin** first came from the bark of the willow tree. Even today scientists are treating **cancer** with something made from a little purple flower called the rosy periwinkle.

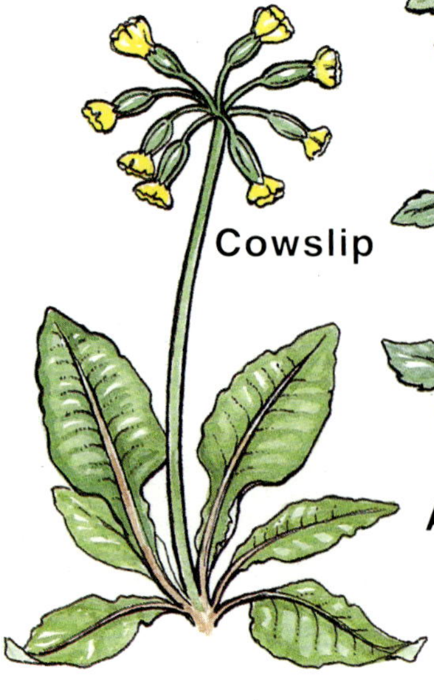

Cowslip

Angelica

The early medicines were known as **simples**. Some people think we should go back to making medicines from plants like angelica, broom, celandines, cowslips, dandelions, violets and even the common stinging nettle!

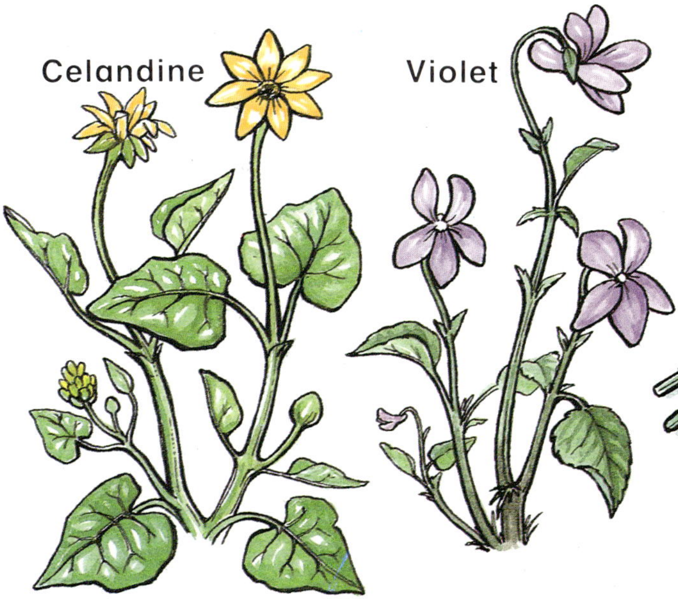

There is no doubt that some of these plants can be helpful, but remember they are also dangerous. Many of them are very **poisonous**. Most medicines are also poisonous if you have too much of them.

Trees

Trees are the giants of the plant world. In fact, the redwood trees of North America are so big that they are called giant redwoods. Some of them are over 100 metres high, and over 2,000 years old!

Every tree has roots, which help to feed it and keep it firm in the ground. The trunk grows up from the roots, and the branches grow out from the trunk. On the branches there are twigs to which the leaves are joined.

Although trees are lots of shapes and sizes they all have these parts.

Can you tell a willow from a horse chestnut, or an oak from a pine? One way to tell is to look at the shape. Trees of the same type usually have the same shape. Another way is to look at the bark. It may be very smooth or it may have ridges.

You can usually recognise trees by their leaves. Every type of tree has leaves that are different. Try feeling the thickness and the surfaces of different leaves. Some leaves are narrow like needles, others are much broader. Some leaves are single, others are made up of lots of smaller leaves on the same stem.

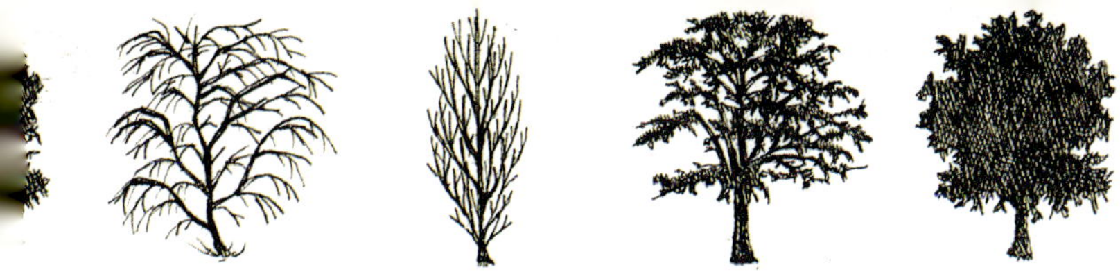

COMPUTER ACTIVITY 2

How old is the tree you know best? Is it 10, 20, or even 50 years old?

You can only really tell the age of a tree after you have chopped it down! The tree has one ring for each year. You can see them on the stump and they are quite difficult to count. Computer Activity 2 gives you the chance to practise counting!

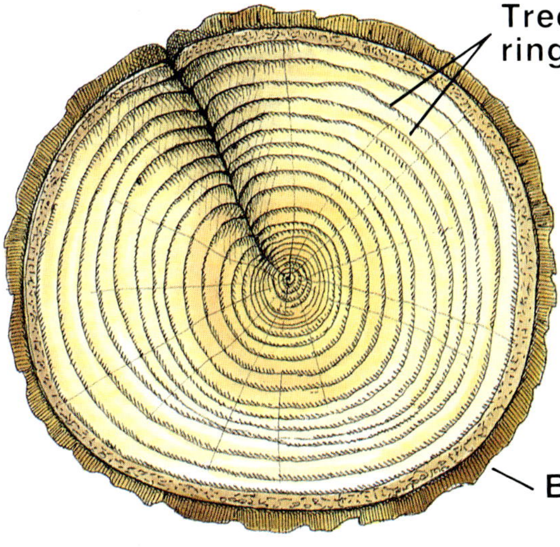

Trees also have flowers or catkins, followed by fruits, nuts, berries, or cones. Some of these are very easy to recognise, but others can be more difficult.

Falling leaves

Some trees lose their leaves each winter and grow new leaves each spring. These trees are called **deciduous** trees.

The leaves stay as buds all through the winter. When the leaves first grow in the spring they are small, soft and yellowy. Later on because of the sun and the rain they become bigger and greener.

In the autumn the leaves dry out and change to beautiful red and golden colours. The cold winds then help to blow the leaves off the trees and they look very bare until the next spring!

Most of the trees with broad leaves which live in countries with freezing cold winters lose their leaves in autumn. The leaves need water as well as sunlight to make food for the tree. In the winter the ground is very cold and the days are very short. The tree cannot keep all its leaves alive.

As autumn approaches a thin layer of cork forms where the leaf stalk joins on to the twig. Water can't get through the cork, and so the leaf dries up and dies.

Leaf rubbing

COMPUTER ACTIVITY 3

Have a look at your chair. Is part of it wood? We use wood for all sorts of things. Before we can use the wood though, the trees have to be cut down.

The little program in Computer Activity 3 lets you chop a tree down! Be careful with the typing - and how you use the axe!

Some hot countries have a long dry season followed by a rainy season. Deciduous trees in these countries shed their leaves at the beginning of the dry season and then grow new ones when the rains start. The trees cannot get enough water during the dry season to keep all their leaves alive.

Evergreens

There are lots of trees that keep their leaves all the year round. They are called **evergreen** trees.

Most trees in cold countries or on mountainsides are evergreens. They often have small tough needles instead of leaves.

The evergreen trees with needles have cones instead of flowers and fruit. They are usually called **coniferous** trees.

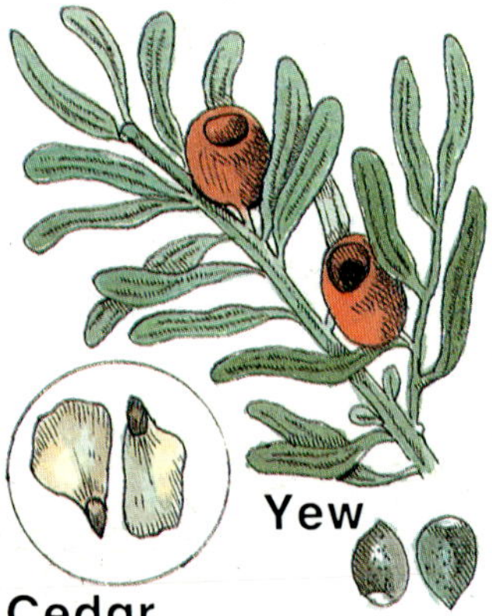

The cones carry the seeds. Some cones are small and soft and they have pollen in them. The wind blows the pollen out. Other cones are hard and scaly; they have a seed underneath each scale. Each seed has a woody 'wing', and when the seed is ripe the wind blows it out of the cone. If it lands in the right place another coniferous tree could grow.

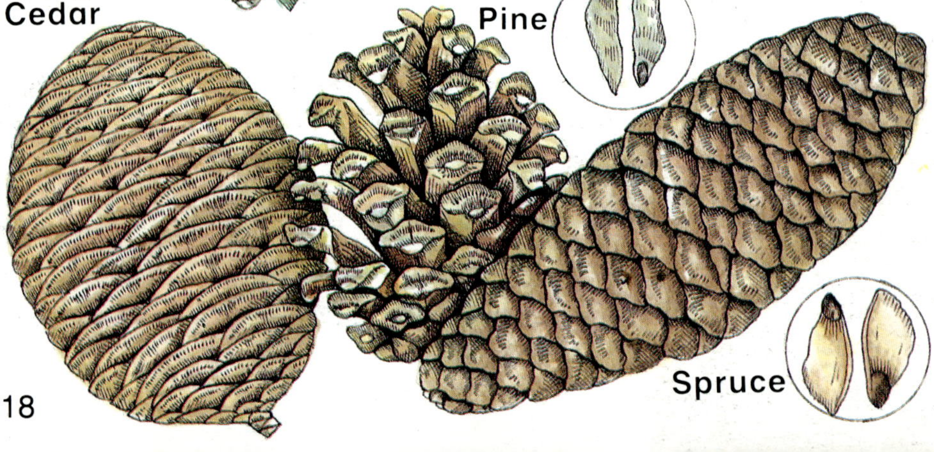

Christmas trees are evergreen trees

Some evergreen trees, such as holly, have broad leaves which are tough and leathery and which the trees keep through the winter. The evergreen trees in hot wet countries are also broadleaved trees. They have many different kinds of fruit and may have flowers and fruit on the tree at the same time.

Flowers and fruits

Some trees have pretty little flowers, like the ash and the beech. Some trees have beautiful flowers, like the apple and the cherry. Their flowers are called blossom and we look for them in springtime.

The hazel, the willow, the alder, the poplar and the oak all have flowers that we call catkins.

The trees in hotter and wetter countries often grow huge, spectacular flowers. The biggest flower ever measured grew in the rainforest of south-east Asia and was over ninety-one centimetres wide.

Many trees have both male and female flowers. It is only when the **pollen** from the male flower reaches the seed in the female flower that they are **fertilised** and can grow. The part of the flower surrounding the seeds becomes the fruit.

Willow catkins

The fruits of trees can look very different. Some are fleshy and good for people and animals to eat, such as apples and cherries. Others are cones, or nuts like the acorn and the conker. Animals like squirrels are important to these trees because they take the fruit to new places where the seeds might be able to grow.

Other fruits have wings or hairs and are carried by the wind. Yet other trees such as the rowan or holly have bright berries which are taken by birds and can be dropped far from the parent tree.

Garden flowers

The flowers that grow in parks and gardens are no longer like the flowers that grow wild in the countryside. People took the wild flowers from the countryside, or brought the plants from other countries, and changed them. Now we have many big brightly coloured flowers in our gardens.

Perhaps the best known garden flower is the rose. There are many kinds of wild rose growing in the world. People collected them, and mixed different sorts together. Now there are more than a thousand kinds of garden rose.

Garden pansy

If you search carefully in the countryside or on waste ground you may find wild flowers which have distant cousins growing in gardens. You probably know the big showy garden pansy with its bright colours, but can you find its little wild relative?

Wild pansy

COMPUTER ACTIVITY 4

Everyone seems to love roses. The poet, Robert Herrick, once wrote:

"Gather ye rosebuds while ye may."

Well now "ye may"! If you haven´t got a garden, or you can´t afford to buy the flowers, you could use the little program in Computer Activity 4. It will make a super bunch of roses!

People make different varieties of the same flower by carefully mixing the **pollen**. They choose flowers that grow well, have a good colour or a delicious scent and they swop the pollen over. This is called **cross-pollination.**

They collect the seeds from the flowers and grow more flowers. Then they mix the pollen again. It all takes a very long time and the people must keep very careful records. Eventually they may grow a new **variety.**

You could try making a collection of drawings or photographs of wild flowers and their garden relatives. Unless they are very common, wild flowers should be left to grow undisturbed. Many plants are rare and in danger of disappearing altogether.

Fruit to eat

Many trees have fruit which is good to eat.
People grow these trees on farms and sell the fruit.

Next time you go shopping look carefully at the fruit in the greengrocers. Can you find out which countries the fruit comes from by looking at the label?

There may be bananas from Jamaica or Honduras.
Pineapples grow there too, and in Africa.
Oranges grow in Spain and Portugal, and apples in Britain and France. But these are not the only places.

Can you think of a fruit for every letter of the alphabet?
There is apple, banana, coconut, date . . .

COMPUTER ACTIVITY 5

Do you like fruit? It is very good for you. Remember that "an apple a day keeps the doctor away".

Did you know that there are hundreds of different fruits. Nearly all of them are really good to eat. Computer Activity 5 tests your knowledge of fruit. You can add things to the program when you discover a new fruit.

Do you know the old saying "an apple a day keeps the doctor away"? Nearly all the fruit we eat is very good for us because it has **vitamin** C in it. A long time ago sailors who went on long voyages became ill with a disease called **scurvy**. Sometimes it was so bad that 3 out of every 4 sailors died. This was because they did not have enough vitamin C.

Scientists discovered that if sailors ate oranges and lemons the scurvy got dramatically better. After that, the British Navy insisted that their sailors should drink lime juice to stop them getting scurvy on long voyages. As a result British people were called Limeys in some countries.

Making a fruit salad

1 Choose lots of fruit

2 Cut up carefully

3 Put in a bowl with juice

Grass, bamboo and thatch

Grass belongs to one of the largest **families** of plants in the world. It comes in lots of different sizes and grows almost everywhere. Many animals eat grass as their main food.

There is meadow grass in the fields of Britain, and prairie grass on the plains of America. There is grass on the mountainside and grass in the forests.

Some grasses are very tall like pampas grass. Others are very short and wiry.

Thatching in England

In some parts of the world straw and hay are still used to make the roofs of houses. This is called thatching. The thatcher sometimes makes special patterns or designs with the top layer of straw. Roofs made of plants can last for many years.

More animals eat grass than any other food. Sometimes they eat the grass out in the field. Sometimes the grass is cut and stored and the animals eat it as hay during the winter months.

In some countries the grasses are bamboos that are so big and strong that people can make their homes from them. They can also make ladders, bridges, water pipes, furniture, walls and floors. Bamboos are the fastest growing plants in the world. Some of them grow about 91 centimetres every day.

Bamboo house in Indonesia

Making hay in France

Cereals

Did you know that every day you eat grass! The plants that we call **cereals** are the most important food in the world. They are all a sort of grass.

The best known cereals are rice, maize and wheat, but there are other cereals like barley, oats and rye. You probably eat wheat everyday. It is made into flour to make bread, cakes and biscuits.

These cereal grasses have to be harvested when the seeds are ripe. In some parts of the world huge machines called combine harvesters cut the crops in enormous fields. In other places people have few machines and must cut the crop by hand.

Perhaps the most important cereal crops in the world are rice and wheat. Rice was first grown in India about 5,000 years ago. Now it is grown all over China, Japan, south-east Asia and in America. Wheat is grown in Europe, Asia and America.

All cereals originally grew in the wild, but people have **cross-bred** them so that now they get far more grain from each plant. People have also bred plants which resist disease and grow well despite bad weather.

In some parts of the world thousands of people starve because their cereal crops fail. Even in a good year they have barely enough grain to feed themselves, and there is none left over to store for the future. Other countries have far more grain than they need and they keep it in huge stores.

COMPUTER ACTIVITY 6

What an awful world it would be without grass and plants.

Computer Activity 6 is all about growing green things. You can have great fun playing with the computer´s keys. When you have tried the program you might like to try making your own picture. It could be made of rice or wheat, grass or bamboo!

WORD LIST

aspirin (page 12) A drug used by doctors to stop mild pain.
cancer (page 12) A horrible disease which stops the body working properly.
carpel (page 9) The female part in the centre of a flower which holds the seeds.
cereals (page 28) These are grasses which have many seeds on each stem and which are good for people and animals.
coniferous (page 18) Trees which have cones instead of fruit, and which have very sharp needle-like leaves are called coniferous trees. Most coniferous trees do not shed their needles all at once each year.
cross-bred (page 28) A variety of plant produced by mixing other varieties together.
cross-pollination (page 23) When the pollen from the male parts of one plant joins with the female parts of another plant.
deciduous (page 16) Trees which regularly shed their leaves or needles all at once are called deciduous trees. This is because the season becomes either too cold or too dry.
digitoxin (page 12) A drug used by doctors to treat heart disease.
evergreen (page 18) Trees which stay green all through the year and do not shed their leaves or needles all at once are called evergreen trees.
fertilised (page 20) A flower in which the male and female parts have joined together so that a seed can develop and grow.
malaria (page 12) An unpleasant fever which can affect people in very hot countries.
morphine (page 12) A drug used by doctors to deaden very bad pain.
poisonous (page 13) Something which makes you feel ill when you eat it, drink it, or breathe it in.
pollen (page 9) A dust produced by the male parts of a flower.
quinine (page 12) A drug used by doctors to treat fevers especially malaria.
scurvy (page 25) A disease caused by not eating enough fresh fruit and vegetables.
sepals (page 9) The outer covering of a flower bud which splits into several pieces to allow the flower to grow.
simples (page 13) Plants that can be used to make medicine.
stigma (page 9) A small stalk on the female part of a flower which catches the pollen.
variety (page 23) A distinct type of one particular plant. For example, 'Queen Elizabeth' is a variety of rose which has very strong stalks and big pink flowers.
vitamin (page 25) Something needed by the body so that it stays healthy.